THIS THING CALLED MONEY

Truth, Lies and Secret you should know about MONEY

GODSON DAUDA

Legal stuff:

This book was created to provide competent and reliable information regarding the subject matter covered. However, it is sold with the understanding that the author and publisher are not engaged in rendering legal, financial, or other professional advice. If other expert assistance is required, the services of a professional should be sought.

The author specifically disclaim any liability that is incurred from the use or application of the contents of this book.

Other Books
by Godson Dauda

Apostasy: *How to know if you're still in the faith*

You too can Dream Big Dreams

Why you must pay attention to Money

9 MONEY secret everyone should know

MONEY from writing E-books: *How & why you should write, lunch and make money from E-books*

Top Secrets on Effective Marketing Strategies (The LODIO of Sells): *simple marketing secret for your business*

Your Skill and Product are Marketable: *12 simple secret strategies you can use to skyrocket your SKILLS AND PRODUCT VISIBILITY*

FREE! To Marry Another

You Too an IDAN: 6 Assured ways to become an IDAN

Free From Money and Success Mediocrity: *A step to success and financial freedom*

6 Online Business you should try
Access this book online by clicking this link:
https://selar.co/m/GodsonE-books.

Dedication

I dedicate this book first to God almighty the giver of life eternal, wisdom and knowledge. And to my late Dad Mr. Dauda Yakubu and my Mum Mrs. Regina Dauda.

CONTENT

Preface

THIS THING CALLED
MONEY

We live in a world were everything is achieved with money. Money is indeed a necessity whether you like it or not.

Some years ago I grow interest to study "This thing called MONEY". And indeed my quest gave me so many answers, that as I am sharing these responses with you today, I am careful not to miss out on any information I had the opportunity to lay my hands on.

Many have shied away and some are still shying away from the reality of Money and its education. Many in the society today are ignorant of what money truly is and I believe you cannot deny the fact of the need to study money, that's why you're reading this book today.

WHY you shouldn't shy away from money...

Is money really important? I defined this mostly in my E-books get them now and have deep insight today. https://selar.com/GodsonE-books.

However let's continue...

Do you know that 90% of the things we do is connected to money? I mean, once you are born, you are groomed to grow and make money. You go to primary school, secondary, university, masters so that your value can increase and you can make a lot more money.

For some of us, we wanted medicine, law or those professional courses so that we can get a job easily and be certain that we will make money too. You see, the Bible acknowledges one thing that men tend to place in their hearts against God. That thing is Money.

You cannot serve two masters; God and Money (Mammon: Covetousness) Money is very important. Lots of laugh, do I even need to say that? If you can, settle the issue of money while you are young like I am trying to. You will also be able to fulfil purpose then. You will be able to help lots of persons.

You should know that, you cannot be so much of help to the poor by being one of them. The most important thing to making money is to know your WHY! In fact, I have come to realize that one of the most important things to define in your journey in Life is your WHY! Most people are concerned with the how. "Godson, how can I make money?" First, WHY do you really need to make money?

I answered this question in this book "why you must pay attention to money" Once you answer your why, the how will be easy. If your why is not strong, no matter the how, you will give up soon. One of my strong WHYs is to never beg for money. I hate begging! Argghh!

Another of my whys is to build churches and promote the gospel. Another is so that I can fund the other aspects of my destiny; Marriage, Family, Charity etc What is your why?

Your WHY could be to travel around the world or to retire your parents to perpetual retirement. It should also be a good and moral reason also that pleases God and also aids to make life on earth easier for others. So, Find a strong why Today!

Let me not bore you on the preface of this book as I am going to be exposing to deep realities on how money works before, today and always. So sorry, if you're not a Christian or believe in the bible reading this book as I will be bringing facts and realities from the Bible to proof the point on how money works.

Your brother
Godson Dauda
A Public Speaker|Music Minister|An Author|Life Coach on: Purpose, Finances, relationship and finding deep spiritual sensitivity

INTRODUCTION

This thing called MONEY! is one of the most controversial topic and many have been misguided and many would be misguided if the wrong information is been shared to them or they keep listening to the wrong information.

One misquoted verse of the bible has been 2 Timothy 2:6-10 Many have been told that "money is the root of all evil" but that's not what the scripture said, I will be digesting that, in this book for more clarity of the passage.

Sincerely we cannot deny the fact, that money is a mammon of the earth and the Bible told us that, "what shall it profit a man to gain the whole earth and loses his soul"Romans 6:23

This thing called MONEY! That have so many views of which some believe that life of mediocrity is not the template of a believer and others believe that everything about their life is MONEY. This kind of people can throw away Jesus or their beliefs a thousand times to pick their dream job all for MONEY.

It is because of this reasons, I feel to some extend many men of God our fathers of faith most especially the evangelicals talk less about these this thing called MONEY. Despite the fact that, they know the need to educate their members on this truth.

This mostly happens because every time the word Rich, prosper, wealth, MONEY is been mentioned, many seems to get irritated especially in church. There's this negative effect or atmosphere that rises even from most well-meaning believers.

I remembered telling someone that I like money and I could imagine the look on his face and his response was ahhh even you man of God and I smiled... and replied, Yes! I like money not love it. The pain and trouble that surrounds this thing called MONEY! Is the most reason why you must talk about it and set ourselves free from this mediocrity beliefs and bondage.

Whether you like it or not "MONEY answered all things"you need this thing called MONEY! For kingdom advancement upon the earth. It is because of money that some are married, some can wake up early and sleep late, it is because of money that we have suicide stories and many walking down the street as beggars, arm robbers, prostitutes, crime increase.

It is because of money and it lack. The wisdom of the poor man who he by his wisdom delivered the city, yet no man remembered him. (Ecclesiastes 9:15-16) you might have a self-denial mentally to say his treasures are stored up in heaven but that's not the case.

We start accepting the fact that his divine power has given us everything we need for life and godliness and I believe in this thing called MONEY!

See we need this thing called MONEY! We need to know how to make, multiply and manage it. Which by His grace as you keep reading this book all will be disclosed.

See, I have come to discover that there are three reasons why everyone of us need money. It is so that we can live a comfortable life and to live a comfortable life you need these things Jesus Christ mentioned in Matthew 6:25 food, shelter which could be cloths and house and also lastly good water.

Take time to think deeply why you want to succeed or have this thing called MONEY! You will see that it evolves around this thing mentioned above especially when your focus is not for kingdom come. And even if it is, the fact still remain that your hustle or existence has been circled around this thing called MONEY!

CHAPTER One

WHAT PEOPLE THINK ABOUT THIS THING CALLED MONEY

Chapter 1

WHAT PEOPLE THINK ABOUT THIS THING CALLED MONEY

There are 2 ways people think when it comes to this thing called MONEY.

According to Toyin Omotsho founder of expertnaire one of the best Affiliate Marketing platform in Africa, "Some people think money is scarce, they think it is only for some special people and some other people think there is plenty of it to go around if you know how to reach out and grab your share.

The unfortunate news is that the majority of people think that money is something that is scarce and that it is greed for them to even think of having plenty of it.

On the other hand, a few set of people are the ones who don't just think that money is plenty. They also believe that they have the ability to attract as many as possible of it for themselves.

Which of these 2 groups do you want to belong to?
Money is one subject that has a sense of irony attached to it. People can't pretend that they don't need money or need the secret to succeed in life. People spend all their entire lives working to get money. Yet, they behave as if getting money is something that is either evil or is of little importance.

There a popular saying that "money is the root of all evil?" It is a saying that was developed and spread by people with a poverty mindset. Meanwhile, the real saying which comes from the bible is that "the love of money is the root of all evil". This means when you love money so much that you want to acquire it by any means possible, it drives you to pursue all sorts of evil means to get it. But there is also another side of the coin that is often not talked about and that is "the lack of money as well is the root of all sorts of evils". Think about it.

A lot of people take to robbery, kidnapping, killing just because they lack money and the only way they think they can get it is by force even when it means attacking other people.

Money Is Not Evil…

One of the beliefs you need to have about money is that it is not evil. Money can't do anything all by itself. It is the handler of the money who determines what it is been used for. For instance, one person might use his money to build hospitals and schools to help other people's lives better. Another person may use the same money to assassinate and harm other people.

It is said that,"money brings out the deep heart desires of a person." In short, if you happen to be an evil person deep inside, you are likely to become more evil when you lay your hands on plenty of money.

At the same time, if you are a good person, you will definitely do more good in life based on your heart desires.

When you understand that money is not evil, you will feel confident in learning about how to attract more money into your life.

When the subject of money or becoming successful is raised, people suddenly freeze up and behave as if you just raised a topic that has to do with killing babies. But really, is it a bad thing to think about getting rich and is thinking about getting rich not a good choice?

Make no mistake about this "thoughts are things". Your consistent thoughts eventually have a way of manifesting in your life. I could go on and on about this but the main lessons I need you to dwell on from this chapter are:

There are two types of mindsets about money and whichever one you choose eventually affects the flow of money to you which might eventually lead to your financial freedom and success. It is either you have a poverty mindset (mediocre) or you have a prosperity mindset.

1. People with prosperity mindset believe that there is a lot of money out there and they also believe that it is theirs. They treat money decently and appreciate other people.
2. People with the poverty mindset believe that money is scarce, they treat and handle money indecently and they hate people who are wealthy which is why they remain poor.

ACTION PLAN: Make a decision today to make yourself prosperity conscious. Get a copy of Think and Grow Rich by Napoleon Hill and start reading.

To further understand the This thing called money, it is important that one understand Money and its movements.

One of the main problems that people have with money is that we often think it is a bunch of special papers printed by the CBN or World Bank.

Why is it that some people have a lot of money sometimes running into billions whereas some other people struggle to even acquire tens of thousands? I leave you to think about that.

Money Mentality

If you're given a N 1000 note, what do you call it? Do you call it money or what?

Majority of people have the mentality that N1000 note is called money. But in Money Mentality and Financial Intelligence N1000 note is not MONEY. It is called Nigeria Currency. You cannot spend N1000 note in London because it's not UK currency, it is Nigeria currency. MONEY IS UNIVERSAL. IT IS NOT A FUNCTION OF ANY REGION. "Money is primarily a medium of exchange or means of exchange." It is a way for a person to trade what he has for what he wants" That means the more exchange a person does to get other people what they want, the more money he/she make. In case you don't understand, this is what it means "Money is a means of exchanging what you have for what you need."

The word CURRENCY is from the word CURRENT, which is something that flows; money is never stagnant. Money flows from those who buy goods and services to those who sell them. This is the pure truth; go all out and stop making excuses, kill that fear, procrastination and laziness.

When you ask the question, "Why are people poor?". Your mind invents excuses. But when you ask the question, "How can people become rich?". Your mind invents solutions. You think value things. Solutions erase problems while excuses worsen problems. This is one of the reasons the rich get richer.

There are 3 Major types of Mentality:
1. Scarcity Mentality
2. Survival Mentality
3. Surplus Mentality

If you will break free from poverty to wealth, you must break free from the Scarcity and Survival Mentality. You have to be someone who has the capacity to add values to people's lives, the capacity to solve problems for people.

To have the capacity to meet needs in people's lives, to solve problems for people, you must have skills. You have got to know how to do something. Not only should you acquire skills, you must develop expertise. You have to become a specialist in what you do. Reno Omokari has this to say and I quite agree with him. He said... "Religion is not a job or a business. Religion is your PERSONAL relationship with God. So, don't fall for the lie that God blesses religious people. God blesses faithful people, because the faithful go out and work, instead of just staying home to pray. And if you have already prayed, fasted and worked hard, and still don't have success, then find a mentor. Christ was not just The Saviour. While He was on Earth, He also Mentored His disciples. Find a mentor who has succeeded (a mentor who has not succeeded is a tormentor).

Follow someone who already knows the way to success." Except you want to involve yourself in an illegal act. If not, even if you fast for 40days and nights, money will not disappear into your account just like that. You must work for it... It's good to have faith but you must apply work to it too...

Most of us get scammed because we want to get rich by doing nothing. Are you kidding me? It doesn't work like that if not, majority if us will have become rich. Someone once said, "certificate will empower you to become a miserable job-hunter".

If you're still in school, the same certificate you are looking for now, Hundreds of thousands of people already have it. Don't rely fully on your certificate or job. They can fail you. But rather rely on God and on yourself because any high income skills you learn now and run a business around it, can't be lost or sacked from you.

It was recorded that in the Last 3 years, 27 Phd certificate holders, applied for truck driver at dangote. You can do your research. That's as at last 3 years. What about last 2 years, or even last year talk less of this year. I don't have to tell you much too.

Thank God we are in the same country. Please, learn an high income skill and start any online legit business as a side hustle.

The Belief System

"Whatever you truly believe, with feeling, becomes your reality" - Brian Tracy. Every one of us acts in a manner consistent with our beliefs, especially the beliefs about ourselves. Your beliefs act like a set of filters that screen our information that is inconsistent with them. You do not necessarily believe what you are, but rather you see what you already believe. You reject information that contradicts what you have already decided to believe, whether or not your beliefs are based on fact or fantasy.

The worst belief you can have are "SELF-LIMITING BELIEF". This exist whenever you believe yourself to be limited in some ways. For example, you may think yourself to be less talented or capable than other. You may think you can go beyond a certain limit because of your family background.

These SELF-LIMITING BELIEFs act like brakes on your potential. They hold you back. They generate the two greatest enemies of personal success - DOUBT & FEAR. They paralyse you and cause you to hesitate to take the intelligent risks that are necessary for you to fulfill your true potential. Will talk more on fear much later.

It is time to challenge every of your self-limiting beliefs because you are made for the top.

Action to Take
1. You have to free your mind from all doubts and fears. Believe you can break all limitations. Believe in your capacity to become the next millionaire that this trying period all over the world. Believe you will make it no matter what may.
2. You have to stand up now and challenge all your self-limiting beliefs that are holding you down. Being it family beliefs or anything.

Develop a success and a financial positive belief system in order to achieve greatness.

CHAPTER *Two*

WHY YOU MUST PAY ATTENTION TO THIS THING CALLED MONEY

Chapter 2

WHY YOU MUST PAY ATTENTION TO THIS THING CALLED MONEY

Everyone needs money, but not everyone needs money. And not everyone want to admit to this very fact. But the truth is, if we do not have money, we cannot afford basic necessities such as accommodation, food and clothing. Still, some people will die from hunger and cold.

Many say money does not bring health and happiness. But when we are ill, we need money to see a doctor. Rich people can afford annual medical check-ups and health supplements. Although money cannot directly buy us health nor happiness, but it can be used to improve our health.

Why do most people love shopping, having a nice meal and watching movies, going for outings, live in a nice and we'll furnished apartment? It is because these activities and environment make them happy. Some say they are happy just talking to their friends. Friendship is valuable, and of course money cannot buy real friends. But it can provide you with entertainment.

But wait!!!

How Much Money?

At some point, you may wonder why money is important and start to analyze the role it plays in your own life. And our society has plenty of different viewpoints when it comes to money and happiness, many see you as a cruel person when you talk about it or call you a money monger.

But much money is truly enough, and how to better with money. I'm sure you have heard many of the different sayings about money too, whether funny or to hit a particular point to make you think. You know the ones, like:

"Money doesn't buy happiness." – Proverb

"Money is the root of all evil." – 1 Timothy 6:10

"Having money isn't everything, not having it is." – Kanye West

The misquoted version ("money is the root of all evil") makes money and wealth the source (or root) of all evil in the world. This is clearly false. The Bible makes it quite clear that sin is the root of all evil in the world (Matthew 15:19; Romans 5:12; James 1:15).

However, when we reflect upon the correct citation of this verse, we see that it is the love of money, not money itself, that is a source of all different kinds of trouble and evil. Wealth is morally neutral; there is nothing wrong with money, in and of itself, or the possession of money. However, when money begins to control us, that's when trouble starts.

But you've probably heard many proverbs, famous quotes, or other sayings from people around you. And while there may be some truth to not let money dictate your entire life and choices, money IS important.

After staying broke and thinking of the thought people have regarding money and seeing them struggling to make earns meet and also lying to their self not to need money for anything, but go about everyday all for this thing called money. I had to came to this conclusion that, the reason money is so important is that it provides options for one to live a better life that he/she choose and puts one in control.

Having money and being comfortable with finances also gives you freedom and options to decide how you want to live and support the things you care most about in your life. This very thought made me came up with a book I titled: "10 shocking reasons you must be Rich and how to do it" watch out for it reason.

So yes, it's true that money cannot necessarily buy you complete happiness forever and greed can make people do terrible things too.

Man ask questions to why is there Evil in this world, or Did God create Evil? Well, this is my take after much study to really comprehend this thoughtful question that, Evil has no existence of its own; it is really the absence of good. For example, holes are real but they only exist in something else. We call the absence of dirt a hole, but it cannot be separated from the dirt. So when God created, it is true that all He created was good. One of the good things God made was creatures who had the freedom to choose good.

And, in order to have a real choice, God had to allow something besides good to choose. So, God allowed angels and humans to choose good or reject good (evil). When a bad relationship exists between two good things we call that evil, but it does not become a "thing" that required God to create it.

Perhaps a further illustration will help. If a person is asked, "Does cold exist?" the answer would likely be "yes." However, this is incorrect. Cold does not exist. Cold is the absence of heat. Similarly, darkness does not exist; it is the absence of light. Evil is the absence of good, or better, evil is the absence of God. God did not have to create evil, but rather only allow for the absence of good.

God did not create evil, but He does allow evil. If God had not allowed for the possibility of evil, both mankind and angels would be serving God out of obligation, not choice. He did not want "robots" that simply did what He wanted them to do because of their "programming." God allowed for the possibility of evil so that we could genuinely have a free will and choose whether or not we wanted to serve Him.

All am trying to point out here is that lack of money is the absent of Money and the absent of money is the absent of 'value'.

Look what the hunger for more wealth and money did to many who has pretended not to have money or want more and how it has ruined their livelihood by investing into scams both offline and online. How on Earth will someone tell you to invest your life savings and you will earn double the amount in an hour's time without telling you or knowing what services they offer?

But while there is truth to some of the negative connotations to money, ultimately you have the strength to dictate how you use money and if you let it control you. Money is not everything in this world, but it can be powerful in helping you achieve your goals and let you make the best of the short life we all have.

CHAPTER Three

QUESTIONS ON THIS THING CALLED MONEY

Chapter 3

QUESTIONS ON THIS THING CALLED MONEY

Q 1:   Does money answers everything?

The statement "Money is the answer for everything" comes in the middle of a section of Ecclesiastes that relates a list of seemingly unrelated proverbs.

Here is the whole proverb: "A feast is made for laughter, wine makes life merry, and money is the answer for everything" (Ecclesiastes 10:19).

The Bible is not teaching here that we should focus on partying and making money; rather, it is making a broader point about wisdom vs. foolishness.

Before we tackle the intent of that specific proverb, let's look at the theme of the book of Ecclesiastes as a whole. In this book, the human author is answering the question "How does one live his or her life apart from God?"

The book is full of worldly wisdom, some of which is good common sense, and some of which is not good or godly at all. One might label the book "How the World Thinks."

A key phrase in Ecclesiastes is under the sun, which is repeated throughout. It indicates that the author is sharing an earth-bound perspective.

He is only considering life "under the sun"; that is, a human life lived to the exclusion of any consideration of God or eternity. From that godless perspective, everything is "meaningless" (Ecclesiastes 1:2, 14).

Ecclesiastes 10:19 and the statement that "money is

18

the answer for everything" is part of a group of observations about wisdom and folly. The behaviors and outcomes of the wise and foolish are being contrasted. For example, Ecclesiastes 10:5–7 presents the error of elevating the foolish to positions of leadership. Verse 10 relates the wisdom of preparation and training.

In regard to interpreting Ecclesiastes 10:19, different commentators take different views: Some see 10:16–20 as the application of the "wisdom-folly" contrast to a nation's leaders. Thus verse 19 says that, even for foolish kings and princes (verse 16), and even for the lazy (verse 18), money makes everyone hear and respond.

If you have money, you have influence and resources: "Money answers to every demand, hears every wish, grants whatever one longs for, helps to all" (Keil and Delitzsch, Old Testament Commentary, 6:779).

In this view, the statement that "money is the answer for everything" is an ancient version of our modern saying "Money talks."

Others see Ecclesiastes 10:18–20 as a separate section and view verse 19 as taking a practical view of money: "At least some money is essential for enjoying life, and steps must therefore be taken to insure that the economy is sound" (Garrett, The New American Commentary, 14:337).

Most likely, "money is the answer for everything" is simply an expression of folly. The proverb mentions feasting, wine, and merry-making as well as money. To the foolish, "it is money that is the answer to everything" (Eaton, Tyndale Old Testament Commentaries, 16:138).

In modern terms, the life of the foolish is circumscribed by partying, alcohol, and money. We see this foolishness play itself out in the world daily. There's nothing new under the sun (Ecclesiastes 1:9).

It is unfortunately true that "money talks" and seems to

be the answer to everything in our world. But wisdom decrees, to the king on down, that the pursuit of riches leads to trouble (see 1 Timothy 6:9–10).

Not all problems can be fixed with money. In the end, Mammon is a hard taskmaster, and only a fool would say, "Money is the answer for everything."

Q 2: Is money evil or its love?

The apostle Paul, in his first letter to his young disciple, Timothy, had this to say: "For the love of money is a root of all kinds of evil. Some people, eager for money, have wandered from the faith and pierced themselves with many griefs" (1 Timothy 6:10). Now this verse is often misquoted as saying, "Money is the root of all evil." Notice how "money" is substituted for "love of money" and "the root of all evil" is substituted for "a root of all kinds of evil." These changes, while subtle, have an enormous impact on the meaning of the verse.

The misquoted version ("money is the root of all evil") makes money and wealth the source (or root) of all evil in the world. This is clearly false. The Bible makes it quite clear that sin is the root of all evil in the world (Matthew 15:19; Romans 5:12; James 1:15).

However, when we reflect upon the correct citation of this verse, we see that it is the love of money, not money itself, that is a source of all different kinds of trouble and evil. Wealth is morally neutral; there is nothing wrong with money, in and of itself, or the possession of money. However, when money begins to control us, that's when trouble starts.

With that said, let's consider the question before us: Why is the love of money a root of all kinds of evil? To help us answer this, we must look at the passage in its greater context. Near the end of the letter (1 Timothy 6:2–10),

Paul is exhorting Timothy regarding the need to "teach and urge these things" to his congregation, "these things" referring back to earlier material in the epistle.

Paul then warns Timothy about false teachers who will seek to warp and pervert the content of sound doctrine for their own greedy gain (verses 3–5). Now notice what the apostle says at the end of verse 5: "Imagining that godliness is a means of gain." These false teachers do what they do for the fame and notoriety they achieve, along with the financial rewards it brings.

Paul wants to steer Timothy away from that trap. In doing so, he tells him the real source of "great gain;" namely, godliness with true contentment (verse 6). Contentment, in a biblical sense, is the recognition that we come into the world with nothing and that everything we have is a gift from God's hands (verses 7–8).

Yet those who desire to be rich (i.e., those who have the "love of money") are the ones who are led into temptation and fall into a snare (verse 9). Paul concludes the passage by telling Timothy that the love of money leads to all sorts of sin and evil.

Simple reflection on this principle will confirm that it is true. Greed causes people to do all sorts of things they wouldn't normally do. Watch any number of TV courtroom dramas, and the crime under consideration is usually motivated by jealousy or greed, or both.

The love of money is what motivates people to lie, steal, cheat, gamble, embezzle, and even murder. People who have a love for money lack the godliness and contentment that is true gain in God's eyes.

But the Bible makes an even stronger statement about the love of money. What we have discussed thus far simply describes the horizontal level of the love of money. In other words, we have only mentioned how the love of money can lead one to commit greater sins against his fellow man. But the Bible makes quite clear that all sin is ultimately against God's holy character (Psalm 51:5).

We need to consider the vertical dimension to the love of money.

In the Sermon on the Mount, Jesus said, "No one can serve two masters, for either he will hate the one and love the other, or he will be devoted to the one and despise the other. You cannot serve God and money" (Matthew 6:24). This verse comes at the end of a passage in which Jesus tells us to "lay up treasures in heaven" (v. 19). Here, Jesus likens a "love of money" to idolatry. He refers to money as a "master" we serve at the expense of serving God. We are commanded by God to have "no other gods" before the only true and living God (Exodus 20:3; the first commandment).

Anything that takes first place in our lives other than our Creator God is an idol and makes us guilty of breaking the first commandment.

Jesus had much to say about wealth. His most memorable conversation about money is His encounter with the rich young ruler (Matthew 19:16–30). The young man asks Jesus what he must do to obtain eternal life, and Jesus tells him to follow the commandments.

When the man tells Jesus that he has done all that, Jesus tests his ability to obey the first commandment and tells him to sell all his possessions and give it to the poor and to follow Him. The young man couldn't do this; his wealth had become an idol it was his master!

After this encounter, Jesus turns to His disciples and says, "Truly, I say to you, only with difficulty will a rich person enter the kingdom of heaven. Again I tell you, it is easier for a camel to go through the eye of a needle than for a rich person to enter the kingdom of God" (Matthew

19:23–24).   This is a hard saying, especially for 21st-century people living in North America. Jesus is saying that wealth is one of the biggest obstacles to coming to faith in Christ.

The reason is obvious: wealth becomes a slave master in our lives and drives us to do all sorts of things that drive us further and further away from God. The good news is that what is impossible for man, entering into the Kingdom of God, is possible with God (Matthew 19:26).

Q 3: Is miracle money real?

Miracle money is money that miraculously appears in someone's purse, wallet, pocket, or bank account to demonstrate the power of God. Preachers who allegedly dispense miracle money claim the power to declare "miracle finances" over those at their miracle money crusades, with the result that some congregants find or receive money instantaneously.

The aberrant practice of proclaiming miracle money into people's pockets is done mainly in various places in Africa by self-proclaimed "prophets" such as Uebert Angel and Shepherd Bushiri.

These men and others teach what is generally known as prosperity theology, the idea that poverty is of the devil (or actually is a demon) and that God wants Christians to be rich and happy and healthy.

Related to the concept of miracle money is the deceptive and manipulative appeal for "seed faith" offerings, which promise a miraculous financial return on a person's money, given in faith to the preacher. Promoters of miracle money point to one of Jesus' miracles as "proof" that what they are doing is of God. On one occasion, when the temple tax was due, Jesus commanded Peter to go fishing and to expect a miracle: "Go to the lake and throw out your line. Take the first fish you catch; open its mouth and you will find a four-drachma coin. Take it and give it to them for my tax and yours" (Matthew 17:27).

The problem is that Jesus' miracle of the coin in the fish's mouth bears little similarity to the modern practice of receiving miracle money. Why didn't Jesus just make the money appear in Peter's pocket? Why didn't angels slip the coin into Peter's hand? Why did Jesus make Peter actually work for the money? Also, the money did not go to either Peter or Jesus but to the authorities for taxes.

Of course, the hucksters claiming the power to produce miracle money for people expect those who are "blessed" in such a way to donate some of the windfall to their ministries. One wonders why the supposed creators of miracle money even need contributions from others. Could they not simply make miracle money enough for themselves? We are warned against those who would take advantage of us in a church setting: "In their greed these teachers will exploit you with fabricated stories" (2 Peter 2:3).

We yearn for our Lord to once again "drive out those who (are) selling" and turn the "den of robbers" back into a "house of prayer" (Luke 19:45–46). God has already given us the greatest gift possible, His only Son, Jesus (John 3:16; Romans 5:8).

God cares about our daily needs and certainly can and will provide for us (Matthew 6:19–34). But we are not immune to trying times (John 16:33; 15:18–25). The apostles and believers in the New Testament church were no strangers to hardship (2 Corinthians 11:21–33; 1 Peter 3:8–17; 4:12–16).

God can use challenging times in our lives to help us grow spiritually (James 1:2–5; Romans 5:3–5). God is more interested in our spiritual prosperity than in our worldly wealth. We cannot serve both God and money (Matthew 6:19–24). Rather, earthly wealth is a resource God entrusts to us so that we might steward it for His good purposes. Those who claim to produce "miracle money" seem far more interested in showmanship, emotional outbursts, and the accumulation of wealth than they do the advancement of God's kingdom.

Believers would be wise to stay away from any person or ministry that claims to produce miracle money.

Q 4: Should I lend money?

God's Word says that many people wander from the faith and pierce themselves with many griefs when they allow money to have an improper hold on their hearts. That's why the Bible contains hundreds of verses on how God wants us to treat money, and this includes the lending of it.

Moses addressed this issue in the Old Testament. Essentially, the Israelites were not permitted to charge interest when they loaned money to an impoverished brother.

They could, however, charge interest on loans made to foreigners. This rule was part of the Mosaic Law: "If you lend money to one of my people among you who is needy, do not be like a moneylender; charge him no interest" (Exodus 22:25; see also Psalm 15:5). This prohibition against charging interest actually included "food or anything else that may earn interest" (Deuteronomy 23:19).

The purpose of the law was two-fold: an interest-bearing loan would only exacerbate the plight of the poor, and God promised a blessing on the gracious lender that would far surpass any interest he would make. Additionally, at the end of every seven years, creditors were to cancel all the debts they were owed by fellow Israelites (Deuteronomy 15:1).

In the New Testament, Jesus tells us not to "turn away from the one who wants to borrow from you" (Matthew 5:42). He applied this principle even to our enemies in their time of need: "But love your enemies and lend to them without expecting to get anything back. Then your reward will be great" (Luke 6:35, emphasis added).

Indeed, there are numerous passages throughout the Bible exhorting us to have a generous and giving heart, especially to the less fortunate. Moses taught his people, "If there is a poor man among your brothers in any of the towns of the land that the LORD your God is giving you, do not be hardhearted or tightfisted toward your poor brother. Rather be openhanded and freely lend him whatever he needs" (Deuteronomy 15:7-8).

The clear teaching of the Bible is that God expects His children to act righteously when lending money. And it helps us to remember that our ability to produce wealth comes from God (Deuteronomy 8:18) and it is God who "sends [both] poverty and wealth; He humbles and He exalts" (1 Samuel 2:7).

Now, there is nothing wrong with legitimately loaning money and expecting to be repaid at a fair rate of interest. Yet we need to remember that the Bible's teaching on money matters also includes borrowing money and indebtedness.

Although the Bible does not expressly forbid borrowing money, it doesn't encourage it, either. It is not God's best for His people, as debt essentially makes one a slave to the lender (Proverbs 22:7). God would rather have us look to Him for our needs than rely on lenders. Additionally, as the psalmist makes clear, we are to repay our debts (Psalm 37:21). When we loan money to someone, we increase that person's debt load and make it easier for him to stumble.

Someone once said, "Before borrowing money from a friend, decide which you need most." There is no doubt that friendships have been strained or even lost due to the lending of money. Yet, if both parties stay within biblical parameters, there shouldn't be a problem.

Nonetheless, to forego jeopardizing a relationship you value, in some situations a gift may be better than a loan. God expects His children to give to those in need, so we give of our time, talents and treasure.

As Jesus taught us, "Give, and it will be given to you. A good measure, pressed down, shaken together and running over, will be poured into your lap. For with the measure you use, it will be measured to you" (Luke 6:38).

Q 5: Is saving money wise?

The Bible teaches that saving money is a wise practice for many different reasons. God is our source and provider for everything we need. "And my God will meet all your needs according to the riches of his glory in Christ Jesus" (Philippians 4:19). One of the main ways God provides for us is through money, and it is our job to steward that money well (Matthew 25:14–27).

We are accountable to God for how we use everything He gives us in this life, including money.

Saving money demonstrates good stewardship of the resources God gives us.

Saving money allows us to be prepared for the future, and being prepared for the future is good. Proverbs 6:6–8 shows us that this principle is lived out even in nature: "Go to the ant, you sluggard; consider its ways and be wise! It has no commander, no overseer or ruler, yet it stores its provisions in summer and its food at harvest." Planning ahead and saving money makes it easier to accomplish goals and allows us to be more effective in ministry (see 1

Corinthians 16:2). When we don't plan ahead and save money, we are more prone to go into debt, which the Bible tells us is unwise (Proverbs 22:7).

Of course, there are plenty of wrong motives for saving money. If we're saving money out of fear of the future, it shows we're not really trusting God to provide (see Luke 12:7; 2 Timothy 1:7). Miserliness is sin, and it's foolish and arrogant to make money our security.

"The wealth of the rich is their fortified city; they imagine it a wall too high to scale" (Proverbs 18:11), yet riches "will surely sprout wings and fly off to the sky like an eagle" (Proverbs 23:5). First Timothy 6:10 warns against greed, saying, "The love of money is a root of all kinds of evil. Some people, eager for money, have wandered from the faith and pierced themselves with many griefs."

To fully understand the value of saving money, we must remember what the Bible says about giving. God desires His people to be cheerful givers (2 Corinthians 9:7).It's impossible to out-give God! "Give and it will be given to you. A good measure, pressed down, shaken together and running over, will be poured into your lap. For the measure you use, it will be measured to you" (Luke 6:38).

Sometimes when God gives us things, be it money or something else, it's intended for us to give away. Other times, He gives us things that are meant for us to keep for ourselves and use in His service and for His glory. It's wise to hold everything God gives us loosely so that we can give it away if He asks us to.

Q6: How much Money is enough?

There is nothing wrong with the pursuit of financial independence and money. But there can be downsides as well.

The issue begins when you let greed consume you and

find yourself doing whatever it takes to make more money. This is when you start to hurt people, alienate friends and family, and end up in a self-destructive path.

The question you have to truly ask yourself is how much money is enough?

For many looking to pursue financial freedom, that number of how much is enough comes to 25x of yearly expenses. So say your expenses are N17,000,000 per year, you'd ideally want to have N425,000,000 saved and invested.

This is the best baseline when evaluating why money is important to you and how much should be enough. It's a good goal and amount where you can live happily and be comfortable in life. For some people, that 25x goal seems like more than enough, not everyone needs to be like Warren Buffett or the next Jeff Bezos. And for others, they would never be satisfied with that amount.

Happiness fades after a certain amount. It's a great idea to have a budget, financial goals, and maybe a net worth number you are striving to achieve. That's never a bad thing! But often it's easy to get into a whirlwind of bad spending habits or needing more and more, never being satisfied with what you have.

In a fascinating research topic, High income improves evaluation of life but not emotional well-being by Daniel Kahneman and Angus Deaton, the authors explore the impact of money on your overall well-being. Essentially, the key findings from their research were that money can keep increasing satisfaction up to any amount, but money only has an affect on your overall happiness up to an annual income of N42,525,000.

While the research goes much more in-depth and is from 2010, something to keep in mind as you pursue money and think about your finances.

CHAPTER *Four*

Chapter 4

THIS THING CALLED
MONEY
MONEY AND MARRIAGE

I might not be married yet, but believe me I have a view of what the bible has to say regarding Money and Marriage. The Bible does not specifically address the handling of money in a marriage, but the principles regarding the relationship dynamics between the husband and wife touch on all aspects of the marriage.

In other words, the principles set forth by the Lord in Ephesians 5:22-33 and Colossians 3:18-19 speak to all facets of the husband-wife relationship.

This means that the spiritual balance of the spousal relationship, in all aspects, is directly impacted by the individual spouse's personal relationship to God. In any relationship there is both blessing by association and suffering by association, and these principles are affected by the choice of each spouse to walk in obedience to the Lord.

Both spouses bring to their union strengths and weaknesses. Molding these individual characteristics into a workable relationship is a matter of understanding the order of God and the gift of grace. Financial decisions that impact the success of the family are a shared responsibility. Whatever the source of God's provisions, whether the result of the husband's employment or the wife's employment or both, the assets accumulated are the responsibility of both partners together as a team.

The important principle in regard to financial

decisions is to "do all to the glory of God" (1 Corinthians 10:31; Romans 14:8; Colossians 3:23-24).

Inherent in the marriage of two people in Christ, however, is the understanding that the husband is the ultimate authority. He is responsible to God to lead and shepherd his family, while his wife's responsibility is to submit to him and be his helper. In the realm of money in a marriage, this could mean that the husband has sole control over the checkbook, pays all the bills, and sees to the family savings and investing as well as giving, while at the same time consulting his wife and getting her input on financial decisions.

It can just as legitimately mean that he delegates this function to his wife, especially if she enjoys or is better suited to the details of the financial realm, and that she takes over the financial details of the "family business." But the husband still has the responsibility to oversee the process. In the end, a couple that works together in the financial aspect of the family will be a couple that usually has good communication and mutual respect.

Finally in the area of money in a marriage, we are also given principles such as the one in Luke 6:38, which states that the more freely we give the greater the blessing.

This means that there is a correlation between the giving that we do as unto the Lord and the blessing that we receive in return, both spiritual and financial. We cannot out-give God.

The more faithful we are in giving back to the LORD, the more we find that what we retain is multiplied and, indeed, more than sufficient to the point of abundance.

CHAPTER Five

WHAT IS
THIS THING CALLED
MONEY ?

Chapter 5

WHAT IS
THIS THING CALLED
MONEY

What is it about this thing called MONEY? That when something happens to it you get uncomfortable or insane. What is it about it?

That when you leave the house without it you quickly return back to pick it (meaning it has the power to send you back home) what is it about it that when you have it you become confident and even boastful?

This thing called MONEY! Can relocate you from one place to another and even force you to marry someone you do not like, eat what you do not like, wear what you do not like and even drink water you do not like.

What is this thing called MONEY? More than just a system "Money is the means used to exchange value (money is not just for spending but for creativity)"

I so much love how my Daddy Joshua Selman defines Money in one of his sermons and am going to be building on those facts and hope you relate.

To understand this called MONEY! There's a need to understand God's design system about Money:

1. To understand money you need to understand time
2. Reward system
3. The concept of destiny.

Not understanding these things you would not understand this thing called MONEY!

Time: The primary aim or assignment of money is as a

tool to help you redeem time and as a tool to make you efficient. That means if you ever claim to have money and you're not able to use it to redeem time and your life does not become efficient you do not use it well.

The Bible tell us in Ephesians 5:17 "to redeem the time, because the day are evil." Meaning anything that stops you from redeeming the time is making you disobedient and you must fit it.

So if you can trek for five hours and you have a car that can take you to where you're going in 5mins, you have redeem time and if you have the car and you can stay comfortably with a driver so can think while you journey that's efficiency that gives you authority and audacity to buy a car without feeling guilty.

Because you are sponsored by a higher motivation, higher than trying to prove a point or show off.

Because we are living in a society that tries to always make we feel guilty for prospering or having this thing called MONEY! Is as if you owe people an explanation.

Money is not just the exchange of value, more than that money is a tool, one of the most effective tools for time redemption.

You can out source the service of others to help you be efficient. You taking your cloths, car is part of redeeming your time to do other things. Every time God brings money your way is not to help you look down on others but to help you live an effective life.

You do not know how efficient your life can be until God truly prosper you or let's say until you have money. Many troubles in our family can be rounded up in peace and in one agreement if there's this thing called MONEY!

Reward System: One thing about this thing called MONEY! Is that the economic system of the kingdom operates on a reward system. In fact, even the world system operates on that, because if I give you money I expect something in return. That's called exchange rate or trade by barter.

One way to live a peaceful life is to be rich or let say have this thing called MONEY, how you may asked? Our lord and saviour taught us "to give to Caesar what belongs to Caesar" Matthew 22:21

Why do you need to give to Caesar what belongs to Caesar and to God what belongs to God. It is because by the time you're serving God and the tribute collectors comes, if you do not have what to give them you will not have peace.

By the time all the bills are piled up e.g. house rent, children fees, what to eat. You will know how important it is to sincerely be rich nothing evil about acquiring wealth and abundance.

What makes it evil is when you forget to seek first his kingdom and righteousness and trust in him to add all the things which has been made available for life and god-liness because it is He who gives wealth. Deuteronomy 8:18.

This thing called MONEY, must be translated with great love and understanding coupled with an open heart to receives it. And watch your life become effective.

It is true that God does not bless us because of what we do. However, the world system does not operate on that it takes only a man who operate and obey the world system and back up by the kingdom principle to operate on that reality.

Destiny Concept: The limit of your destiny is time and whatever you give your time to is the limit of your destiny. Do you know spending your time chasing after money could be a curse? Well you might believe it or not but that's a fact.

MONEY was never designed to be a life-long pursuit. It was Joshua Selman (Apostle) who once said, "if you become successful at 80,90 it not a testimony", and that Jesus finish his assignment at 33 and we have remain benefactors of the speed in his life.

Well it true but I also think whether you become successful at 25 or 52 its still a testimony. There's a thing called time and chance. It is different smoke for different people. Time and chance happens to them all. Ecclesiastes 9:11.

However, that is should not give room for procrastination caused by a stagnant spirit of failure. You ought to break barriers open your eyes and heart to opportunities around you there will always be no job.

But there's this thing in Africa that if we do not break it, it will continue. "it is called the cause of late achievement" when a young man in Africa prospers at age 22, 23.

People will say something is wrong, but at 40, 50 so they say yeah... that's how we are. May that never be your portion.

THE SECRET OF
THIS THING CALLED
MONEY

Chapter 6

THE SECRET OF
THIS THING CALLED
MONEY

I grew up in a fairly financially literate household.

My dad was a serial entrepreneur with a high tolerance for calculated risk, and my mom was the more conservative one who had a mind for resourcefulness. In short, my dad earned and my mom saved, and they made a great match for each other (and for their kids to learn from).

I have also stayed with my grandparents who I observed almost the same kind of system. And even with this (what I believe to be comparatively uber-healthy relationship to money compared to what a lot of people grow up with as financial role models), there were still some things that I wish I had been taught much younger about money (or taught at all).

Not to go too far down the conspiracy theory hole here... but the more disempowered we are when it comes to our relationship to money, the more controllable we are. The more controllable we are, the easier it is to convince us that we're defective, and need a solution to our inherent brokenness.

Everyone has their stuff when it comes to money. It's such a loaded topic because, in a society that values productivity and achievement above all else, it's so easy to conflate our net-worth with our self-worth.

Over the last decade I have had the great fortune of having some truly remarkable mentors (and clients) who had such bulletproof money mindsets that a lot of their wisdom has rubbed off on me through the years. So, without further ado, here are the nine things I wish someone had taught me about money in my teen years, so that I could have had an earlier leg up in life.

The money you make matters, the money you save matters

An often passed around sentiment is that "It's not about how much money you make, it's about how much you save." And while this is valuable advice for a good percentage of the world that overspends and lives beyond their means, it isn't an either/or equation, but rather a both/and. Yes, saving money matters, but so does your income. An expert saver who makes $20,000 per year will generally not save as well as someone who is an okay saver who makes $500,000 per year. The income you generate through your work is important, and so is how much of that you are able to hold on to and invest. Both sides of this equation require effort and discipline.

It can require effort to let go of your mental blocks to money and discipline to put in the effort that allows you to call money into your life. It also requires effort and discipline to not then immediately turn around and spend all of your earnings on a new pair of thousand dollar sneakers every week.

I will go deeper into both sides of this equation at multiple points throughout this book just I have so far.

Time is more important than money

The following is a true story. There once was a local fast food restaurant that put out an offer online that said, "If you print this coupon off and come in to this location, you can get a burger for free. Absolutely free. No strings attached. Valid today only." The burger was roughly valued at $6. Local residents would not confirm or deny if the burger was as delicious as this one. Within the hour, hundreds of people were lined up outside of the restaurant, and the line was so long that they packed themselves in covering more than four city blocks. Now, everyone loves a good deal, and I get that.

But if you zoom out for half a second and think about it rationally... many of these people were waiting more than two hours to get their 'free' burger. So if you do the basic math, they were valuing their time at approximately $2-3 per hour. I bet that if you asked those same people if they would sit on your drive way and do absolutely nothing for $2 an hour, most of them would say no (well, at least I hope that would be the case).

But that's exactly what they were doing. Instead of coming in the next day and spending $6 and getting their food in three minutes, they were willing to wait two to three hours to get it. This true story is a microcosm of how people relate to time and money. People with unhealthy money mindsets disproportionately overvalue their money, and undervalue their time.

With all of the money mentors that I have worked alongside over the last years, the exact opposite has always been a faster ticket to financial freedom. Don't be so married to holding on to your precious Money at all costs (pun intended), and be more aware of how you invest your time on a day to day basis.

If you don't like a book you're reading, stop reading it. If you can't stand the movie you're watching, leave the theatre. If you find yourself feeling completely drained after hanging out with your friends, and this has been a pattern for months or even years, then change your social circle. Bulk-buy certain things that you know you will be using long-term (toilet paper, toothpaste, salt, etc.), again, not for the dollar savings as much as the time you save by not having to go pick it up whenever you run out.

Your time matters. You can always make more money, but you can't generate more time. So treat it as the precious commodity that it is. A popular adage in Nigeria says, "time na money."

Be roughly aware of where your money goes

It isn't necessary to know where every single dollar goes. You don't need a super detailed monthly spreadsheet accounting for every outgoing cent. But it is important that you have a general finger on the pulse of

a) where your money goes, and

b) b) approximately in what volume.

I have known people who accounted for every money, and I think that this level of detailed attention quickly leads to anxiety and scarcity thinking. And I have also known people (many more people, compared to the previous example) who completely turned a blind eye as to where there money went for years. And while it is good, on one level, to generally trust that money flows in and money flows out, having no sense of what your monthly expenses are is a one-way ticket to broke-dom.

You can use an app like Mint, or just put all of your expenses on your debit and credit cards, and then look at your statement at the end of the month. Are you surprised by what you see? Do you spend more on entertainment/food/clothing/transportation than you assumed?

The point isn't to make yourself wrong. Simply having the rough number in your mind as to what you have already been spending is enough of a start. Then, if you want to start making small and gradual adjustments as to where your money goes from that place of awareness, you are free to do so.

Focus more on value creation than you do on penny pinching

Most money advice focuses too much on saving. Not buying your morning coffee at Starbucks or Chicken republic might save you $100 that Is N100,000 a month. But it isn't going to make you rich. If your goal is saving a significant amount of money, creating massive value for the world matters more than cutting costs. I think of it like this.

You can't control the direction the wind is blowing, but you can create a bigger sail in order to catch more momentum for your boat to coast with. Sure, put some energy towards cutting costs. Negotiate your monthly phone bill down $20/month that is N20,000 if it's easy enough to do. Make your own breakfasts instead of eating out every morning.

But most of your wins will come from the unlimited upside of the equation, which is creating more value for the market place. Which leads us to.

You can always become more valuable to the market

Abraham Lincoln was quoted with saying, "Give me six hours to chop down a tree and I will spend the first four sharpening the ax." Or, how this is relevant in money terms, there's no way that you can double the amount of hours that you have in a day with which to work, but there is a way in which you can double the value that you bring to the marketplace. This is that whole 'work smarter not harder' thing you've probably heard before. Except instead of working in a more intelligent manner, it's about becoming more as a person.

Get your master's degree. Start a new business. Put out a new product. Find a way to sharpen the ax that is you.

Add more value, receive more value money, making money, saving money, money advice Your technique is terrible, Aidan. Or, as Zig Ziglar once said, "You can have everything in life you want, if you will just help other people get what they want."

Focus less on ways that you can find and generate money, and think more about how you can either help more people (scale) or help the people that you're already helping that much more (depth/impact).

This overall mindset shift also lends itself to the idea of being a life long learner. As long as you are growing, learning, and giving more, you will never want for anything. It is only when your mind collapses into a selfish, constricted state that it convinces itself that money is a scarce resource that must be conquered and hoarded.

Reward yourself

If you're a parent and you're going on a long road trip, eventually your kids (who are sitting patiently in the back seat) will become bored and will start asking "Are we there yet?"This is how your subconscious mind/inner child works when it comes to saving a good amount of money. If you delay gratification and do a good job of building wealth, but you never reward yourself, your inner 'kids in the backseat' will grow tiresome and start revolting.

Many of my clients are what I would consider to be super-earners (making anywhere from $3-200 million dollars per year), and this is a common trap that they can fall into. Discipline is a valuable skill to have in your tool belt. But if it isn't offset with occasional fun, play, rest, or reward, then the soul dries up and you will feel depleted and/or resentful.

So make sure you're rewarding yourself along the path to keep your full self engaged and aligned in the process.

Rewards are always highly individual. What is a reward to some is a punishment to others. So make sure you're regularly checking in with yourself and asking 'What does the carrot on the end my stick need to look like for me to stay motivated in this journey?'

Get rich slowly with long-term investing and thinking

Just like most people value their money more than their time, in my experience, the majority of people also think in too short of a timeline. They want to get rich quick. They want investment opportunities that will make them instant millionaires. They want to know how to start businesses that can generate crazy amounts of cash from day one. Without fail, all of the most successful super-earners I know got to where they are through hard work, consistent effort, and patience.

As Conor Oberst, of Bright Eyes fame, once sang, "I'd rather be working for a pay cheque, than waiting to win the lottery."Money is energy, and energy wants to move. So sitting money is dead money. With this in mind, sitting on a large amount of money and just having it collect dust in your chequing account is a guaranteed way to lose money as inflation will be whittling away at your savings.

While there are times when sitting on a pile of liquid capital is a smart choice (when you think we're on the precipice of a recession, when you're waiting to invest in undervalued stocks, when you're about to buy a business, etc.), by and large, you want your money making money for you.

Anyone who has spent even an hour learning about investment strategy has likely heard the term compound interest. This is when you invest money, the addition of interest to the original amount of money occurs on top of the principal amount, and then you earn interest on the principal sum plus the interest. This effect compounds with time, and you make money on top of your earned money.

So if you invest $100,000 in an account that nets you 10% returns year over year (without investing a dollar more), then after a decade your $100,000 turns into $259,374. If you are able to let that amount sit for another decade, then that amount accumulates to an amount just shy of $700,000. So this stuff adds up fast.

You are the most important asset you could ever invest in

Last and certainly not least, the most valuable asset you could invest in is yourself. Warren Buffett, one of the grandfathers of modern investing once said, "The best investment you can make is in your own abilities."

If there's a mentor that you want access to but you have to pay, then pay. If there's a mastermind group that has a financial requirement to join, pay that too. If there's a program, a training, or a workshop that you know will be good for you but it costs money, pay that money and make it happen.

Again, people are too stingy with their money and not stingy enough with their time. The right coach, counselor, or mentor can literally shave years off of your learning curve if you are open to receiving their gifts (and paying for those gifts).

I have invested tens of thousands of dollars in mentors, coaches, therapists, and experts over the last fifteen years, and I have never regretted a single dollar spent. In fact, I can attribute all of my greatest growth surges (in terms of personal fulfillment and financial mastery) to times where I anted up and put my money where my mouth is.

So if you're holding back on investing on yourself because it costs money, I would encourage you to look at that and second guess it. Think of all the time, energy, and effort it could require to try to learn it on your own. And then think about how much sooner you could be out of pain and into pleasure once you commit yourself fully.

Invest in yourself first. You'll be glad you did.

THE REAL BENEFITS OF
THIS THING CALLED
MONEY

Chapter 7

THE REAL BENEFIT OF THIS THING CALLED

MONEY

While your whole life does not need to focus on money and accumulating wealth, it is still important to dedicate your time to understanding it and building a strategy.

Look, we all know that more money means you can generally afford a fancier lifestyle, bigger homes, better vacations, and flashier cars. But those material items are not the real benefits of having money and the temporary excitement from those items quickly wanes.

So why is money important?

Money Gives You Freedom
Money is important because it gives you the freedom to do what you want, when you want, where you want. Someone call this "FU Money," which means you reach a point where you can just walk away from a job you hate and are not reliant on anyone's financial support.

So many troubles we have in our homes or Churches is mostly because of lack of stable finance.

I remember, I once had to quit a Job because it stole my freedom to do anything in serving God and having the privilege to mingle and fellowship with other person's around.

Do you have hobbies you want to pursue? A dream to start your own business? Money gives you the freedom to explore those areas and take a bit of risk.

49

Money Gives You Options

Being able to make choices and have options is one of the best feelings in the world. Knowing you are stuck in a particular situation because you need the money or financial help is frustrating, so removing that from your life is a great relief.

When you have money, you control what you want or don't want to do. Want to have a different career? Want to move to a different state or country? Want to travel somewhere new for vacation? Do it.

Money Creates Financial Security

One of the most powerful feelings you can have is knowing you do not need to worry about money. Financial stress is a common problem among people and families, which can lift a huge burden.

Whether you lose your job or some economical turmoil happens, you aren't worried about paying bills, paying to see a doctor for medical reasons, or wondering where your next meal will come from.

Having money and having a financial plan creates more security for you and your family.

Money Can Create More Life Experiences

Life is short and goes by fast, which means you should want to experience the best things life has to offer while you are here.

Hoarding money and never experiencing anything is a waste, after all you can't take the money with you to the grave! While that might not paint a pretty picture, it's completely true.

When you have money, it creates opportunities for you to get more out of life, travel the world, try new things, and get out of your own bubble of where you live. This can also help drive more happiness overall as you are experiencing more that life has to offer.

Money Helps You Give Your Family More

While generational wealth can be a good thing, there is a fine line of instilling in your children good values and work ethics beyond just handing money over to them. But money matters because you can provide your family and you with better education opportunities, better healthcare, and a better start in life overall.

There are plenty of children that become spoiled and it creates unrealistic expectations of money while growing up. But that's where teaching them about money and not giving them every little luxury without hard work will be key.

Money Lets You Give Back

At some point, you may reach a level of income or financial freedom where you can afford to give back. Helping out charities, your local community, or other causes is a great feeling and it can create happiness when you are helping others.

To me I feel this one of the greatest reason why I desperately need to make money or attract this thing called money.

Those are some of the main reasons money is important and should be things you think about in your own pursuit of financial independence. But I'm sure there are other reasons money might be important to you as well.

THE NEGATIVE SIDE OF THIS THING CALLED MONEY

THE NEGATIVE SIDE OF THIS THING CALLED MONEY

While there are plenty of benefits to having money, there are negatives to it as well. Focusing your energy on making money, saving, and investing is important but it's a careful balance to not let it consume every little decision you make. Before I share points on the negative side of money let me share briefly on why is the love of money the root of all kinds of evil?

The apostle Paul, in his first letter to his young disciple, Timothy, had this to say: "For the love of money is a root of all kinds of evil. Some people, eager for money, have wandered from the faith and pierced themselves with many grief's" (1 Timothy 6:10).

Now this verse is often misquoted as saying, "Money is the root of all evil." Notice how "money" is substituted for "love of money" and "the root of all evil" is substituted for "a root of all kinds of evil." These changes, while subtle, have an enormous impact on the meaning of the verse.

Remember, I said something about this earlier. Its means this passage has an important view on the subject matter we have here. The misquoted version ("money is the root of all evil") makes money and wealth the source (or root) of all evil in the world. This is clearly false. The Bible makes it quite clear that sin is the root of all evil in the world (Matthew 15:19; Romans 5:12; James 1:15).

However, when you reflect upon the correct citation of this verse, you see that it is the love of money, not money itself, that is a source of all different kinds of trouble and evil. Wealth is morally neutral; there is nothing wrong with money, in and of itself, or the possession of money. However, when money begins to control us, that's when trouble starts. With that said, let's consider the question, Why is the love of money a root of all kinds of evil? In other to have a deep understanding on the negative side of money.

This is not to say money is not important so as not to contradict my above points on why money is important. Now to understand, why the love of money a root of all kinds of evil. we must look at the passage in its greater context.

Near the end of the letter (1 Timothy 6:2–10), Paul is exhorting Timothy regarding the need to "teach and urge these things" to his congregation, "these things" referring back to earlier material in the epistle. Paul then warns Timothy about false teachers who will seek to warp and pervert the content of sound doctrine for their own greedy gain (verses 3–5).

Now notice what the apostle says at the end of verse 5: "Imagining that godliness is a means of gain." These false teachers do what they do for the fame and notoriety they achieve, along with the financial rewards it brings. Paul wants to steer Timothy away from that trap. In doing so, he tells him the real source of "great gain;" namely, godliness with true contentment (verse 6).

Contentment, in a biblical sense, is the recognition that we come into the world with nothing and that everything we have is a gift from God's hands (verses 7–8). Contentment must be understood with a good perspective presented in the Bible as seen above. Contentment is not an excuse or license to laziness, procrastination and fear to go out there and attract this thing called money with your God given abilities and developed values.

Yet those who desire to be rich (i.e., those who have the "love of money") are the ones who are led into temptation and fall into a snare (verse 9). Paul concludes the passage by telling Timothy that the love of money leads to all sorts of sin and evil. Simple reflection on this principle will confirm that it is true. Greed causes people to do all sorts of things they wouldn't normally do. Watch any number of dramas, and the crimes under consideration is usually motivated by jealousy or greed, or both.

The love of money is what motivates people to lie, steal, cheat, gamble, embezzle, and even murder. People who have a love for money lack the godliness and contentment that is true gain in God's eyes. But the Bible makes an even stronger statement about the love of money. What we have discussed thus far simply describes the horizontal level of the love of money.

In other words, we have only mentioned how the love of money can lead one to commit greater sins against his fellow man. But the Bible makes quite clear that all sin is ultimately against God's holy character (Psalm 51:5). We need to consider the vertical dimension to the love of money.

In the Sermon on the Mount, Jesus said, "No one can serve two masters, for either he will hate the one and love the other, or he will be devoted to the one and despise the other. You cannot serve God and money" (Matthew 6:24). This verse comes at the end of a passage in which Jesus tells us to "lay up treasures in heaven" (v. 19). Here, Jesus likens a "love of money" to idolatry. He refers to money as a "master" we serve at the expense of serving God. We are commanded by God to have "no other gods" before the only true and living God (Exodus 20:3; the first commandment). Anything that takes first place in our lives other than our Creator God is an idol and makes us guilty of breaking the first commandment.

Jesus had much to say about wealth. His most memorable conversation about money is His encounter with the rich young ruler (Matthew 19:16–30).

The young man asks Jesus what he must do to obtain eternal life, and Jesus tells him to follow the commandments. When the man tells Jesus that he has done all that, Jesus tests his ability to obey the first commandment and tells him to sell all his possessions and give it to the poor and to follow Him. The young man couldn't do this; his wealth had become an idol it was his master!

After this encounter, Jesus turns to His disciples and says, "Truly, I say to you, only with difficulty will a rich person enter the kingdom of heaven. Again I tell you, it is easier for a camel to go through the eye of a needle than for a rich person to enter the kingdom of God" (Matthew 19:23–24). This is a hard saying, especially for 21st-century people living in blind pursuit for wealth and power. And have come to discover that, the absolute way to knowing God's will for our lives is total submission to him. Proverbs 3:5-7 said, "Trust in the LORD with all thine heart; and lean not unto thine own understanding. In all thy ways acknowledge him, and he shall direct thy paths. Be not wise in thine own eyes: fear the LORD, and depart from evil."

Jesus is saying that wealth is one of the biggest obstacles to coming to faith in Christ. The reason is obvious: wealth becomes a slave master in our lives and drives us to do all sorts of things that drive us further and further away from God. The good news is that what is impossible for man, entering into the Kingdom of God, is possible with God (Matthew 19:26).

Now, here are some of the negative point to money.
Obsessing Over Money Causes Problems
While we may all strive for money or financial peace, obsessing over money and making money can really cause problems in your life.

When you focus all your time on money and trying to acquire more of it, you can end up destroying your relationships with family and friends. It can also lead you down a path of unethical behavior (see once again, criminal activities just to get more money.

Having an obsession with money is a destructive disorder that can ruin your life and others. Sure, you may have all the money in the world, but if you trampled over everyone, who is going to be next to you enjoying life?

No one or not anyone that you would trust to genuinely care about you and not your wealth.

Making Money Can Cause More Stress
Not only can money help reduce financial stress, but it can also cause more unwanted stress too. Funny how that works, aren't it?

For those where money is never enough, no matter how much they have it actually can create more stress.

You find yourself working crazy hours every week, spending every waking moment thinking about money, and even getting anxious over your efforts for more. That stress not only takes a toll on your mental and physical health but affects those around your like family and co-workers.

Can Create More Family Disagreements

According to a MarketWatch article, they mentioned that TD Ameritrade found that 41% of divorced Gen Xers and 29% of Boomers say they ended their marriage due to disagreements about money. These facts may not be far from you now as you're reading this book. While these numbers are just a few years old, money continues to be a common cause for disagreements and arguments among spouses and families.

If you are not on the same page with your spouse or family, money will certainly be a common friction point. And you certainly won't be in agreement ALL the time, but having similar values and thoughts about money can limit the disagreements.

CHAPTER *Nine*

THE 3Ms OF
THIS THING CALLED
MONEY

How to attract, multiply and manage Money

Chapter 9
THE 3Ms OF
THIS THING CALLED
MONEY

How to attract, multiply and manage Money

I will be revealing a lot in this chapter of the book but before I share with you on the 3 M of Money: how to make, multiply and manage money permit me to share with you on one very important key of making money.

By creating multiple streams of passive income. You see, there are two major streams of income.

Active and Passive. Both of them are very important.

Active income requires you to work on your job daily or business. In active income, your time is tied to your money. Active income is good but it is not the best form of income.

The ogakpatata(the real boss of all) of them all is passive income. Passive income is making money from early investment of money or time.

First, you put in the efforts and you sit down and watch the money roll in. Like my prof. Will say, "Your money can never be massive until your money becomes passive!" Akpe Emmanuel

Another quote Akpe Emmanuel also said that, "Until you make money while sleeping, you don't have any business spending long hours sleeping"Akpe Emmanuel (2018)

Now, what are some examples of passive income?
1. The easiest form of passive income is supplementary businesses. That is, leveraging on an existing business with traffic and customers to sell your own products.

60

For example, If someone is selling akara, approach the person and drop bread for her to also sell on your behalf. Simple. That's just the basic example. I didn't ask you to go and sell bread sha.

This is creating alliance with an already existing business. Leveraging on their customers, time and efforts. I did this to my mum's provision store at age 16. There are lots of businesses to leverage on, just look around you and form a relationship ASAP.

2. Train a group of people and outsource jobs to them. I have people I've given jobs to. Others have security outfits, private lesson outfits. Can you gather people to do a job without your presence?

    This is also known as the agency method. If you are good at what you do and you have lot's of clients coming in, get people and outsource it to them. You will be sleeping and making money.

3. Rental businesses. Rental business is very passive. There are lots of things you can rent out. Projectors, sound systems, books, chairs. If funds are available, build houses and keep it on rent or even event centres. Whatever you can rent, it will be passive.

4. Write books, sing songs or anything that can bring royalties. Amazon is a great platform for publishing books and Selar too. You can make an income for life by writing and publishing your books there.

    Just invest few hours to create any ebook and you can get passive income coming in. you chat me for more on this or google my book "Money from writing Ebooks"

5. You can also invest in stocks and shares, bonds and

treasury bills. If you know financial vehicles well, you can make passive income investing there. This is not for everyone. In fact, if you don't have good money, don't get in. There's a big difference between the 10% of 100,000 naira and that of 10 million naira.

Finally, Always look for ways to turn your active income into passive income. Financial freedom happens when your passive income exceeds the cost of your lifestyle. (The quote I told you about). Then you can travel and live as you want. Without having to depend on anyone for money. Now....

HOW DO YOU ATTRACT, MULTIPLY AND MANAGE MONEY?
You attract money by.....

1. Developing a skills that is having a value that men will seek, competence and attention: It depends on who you are before the money follows. One has to be developed personally, concentrate on being the best version of yourself. It is based on who you are and not what you do you get money, one should grow and develop by so doing he gets power (power to take action, power to control the money). One should focus on improving themselves and the money will come naturally.

Financial intelligence is important. People tend to chase money without knowing the Dynamics of it, one needs to attract money by knowing and learning how it works.

To get money is not easy and people think doing easy stuff will get them rich. One has to grow from the inside, work hard and the results will come later. It's not by doing easy things, one has to make sacrifices and pay for it with hard work, the end results will become easy (Life becomes easy).

The mindset of an individual is very important, one has to make up his mind to strive hard so as to rest later. The mindset is to focus on achieving difficult tasks and then easy task will be fixed later. With challenges comes success.

One should be a master of a skill. They are different professions which can take years to master it but with skills it takes shorter period and you become a master of it. You need to choose the right skill to get positive results. To get to your destination one picks a vehicle that will be suitable for the journey so also skills, with the right skill in hand, you get your destination with positive results.

If you are a master of any skill or field, you don't beg for money because the money follows you when you're good at what you do. Based on skills you are good; having positive results, people will come to you naturally. To become a master takes competence, confidence; it takes patience, it doesn't happen in a day or month you work hard; keep learning; apply and grow in the skills continuously.

Focus on it. Do not jump from one skill to another, let people know you are the master of that field. Take authority over it, you should be remembered for your field and to be remembered for your field you need to work hard. With competence comes money naturally.

One needs to be courageous and also be bold to take hard steps. Leave your comfort zone and strive hard. One needs courage to market his products, you don't have to be very rich to be courageous. In whatever you do, be bold about it. One has to be committed to what he's doing. You shouldn't be off and on about your skill or business. We should always be consistent.

Whatever skills or business one is into, put in your best in it; be committed and consistent. From consistence comes competence and from competence comes mastery. Being committed leads to success of skills and business.

One has to have a saving habit. Saving is very important in the aspect of money. One shouldn't squander money because he is having much today. You save money today, and it will save you tomorrow. Saving is a habit. You save to become rich. One shouldn't save money just to pile up cash but to make use of it to make more capitals.

Money attracts more money. You save money before spending, decide to keep some percentage and after keeping the percentage; the remaining balance should be for spending. Earn more money and also save more! It is important to invest money and multiply. The best way is to invest in yourself, even when there are challenges one bounce back easily.

Invest your money on businesses, stocks and even real estate. Whatever you invest your money into, one should have a knowledge about it. One should study the business, investigate on it and when satisfied with the results he can invest into it. You will always be wealthy when you invest your money.

One should be with the right association. Connecting with you right associations attract great opportunities. Even when we don't have them as friends, hang out with them on social media (follow their handles and you get to see the things they do, how they go about their businesses; interviews and so much more).

You can learn from their actions and see how their mindsets works. Hang around people who are not broke and fly with the eagles. Leverage is important, using minimum efforts to get maximum results. With leverage, stuff are done the easy way with less energy. One doesn't have to start from the scratch, use the available information and minimize your mistakes that use of Internet. Use the internet.

God bless you so true people so we shouldn't look down on them. We should value every single relationship. One connection can change our financial level. When we meet people, seek to add value to them first and you will gain favor when the time is right.

Prompt action - people have great ideas of business but claim they are waiting for the perfect time to start. When one has the idea ready for the business, start! You don't have to wait, get started with it and make corrections on the way. If one keeps waiting someone might end up doing your business idea.

Lastly, Knowledge is important so also action. Action brings out distinction. Put whatever you learn into action and you get results from your acts.

2. Excellence: You attract even more money by been excellent at what you do. Excellence they say, is the quality of excelling, of being the very best at something. Human beings have an intrinsic desire to see excellence. In every people group across the world, excellence is prized and rewarded.

Whether it is a tribe celebrating excellence in hunting or a Wall Street accountant promoted because of his excellence in finance, our appreciation of excellence comes from our Creator.

To be made in God's image means that He imparted some of His character qualities to us (Genesis 1:27). We crave justice because He is just (Psalm 9:16). We love because He is love (1 John 4:16). And we strive for excellence because He is excellent in everything He does (Deuteronomy 32:4). Many things get in the way of human excellence, including apathy, carelessness, and laziness. Our sinful nature is that part of us that is unlike God and is in fact in opposition to God and His excellence.

We are all born sinners, and that sin manifests itself in a thousand ways. We cut corners, we shirk, we settle for second best (or third or fourth best) if the effort to achieve excellence is more than we're willing to give.

God's cure for our careless ways is to remind us that He is our ultimate judge. We must answer to Him for how we spend our time, our resources, and our energy (Matthew 12:36; 1 Corinthians 3:13–15). Striving for excellence should be a part of all we do: "Whatever you do, work at it with all your heart, as working for the Lord, not for human masters, since you know that you will receive an inheritance from the Lord as a reward. It is the Lord Christ you are serving" (Colossians 3:23–24).

Knowing that it is Christ Himself we are serving, we don't want to present Him with anything but excellence. Whether it is sweeping streets or running a country, we should strive for excellence in work ethic, in character, and in craftsmanship. No one is good at everything, but we're all good at something. God expects us to develop the skills and gifts He's given us in order to serve Him and others better.

Paul addressed the subject of excellence in Romans 12:6–8: "We have different gifts, according to the grace given to each of us. If your gift is prophesying, then prophesy in accordance with your faith; if it is serving, then serve; if it is teaching, then teach; if it is to encourage, then give encouragement; if it is giving, then give generously; if it is to lead, do it diligently; if it is to show mercy, do it cheerfully." In other words, find your gifts and use them with excellence.

Joseph is an example of a young man who did his best at everything he was given to do. Even when Joseph was unjustly imprisoned, he was able to impress the warden with his excellent character and work ethic (Genesis 39:1–2, 20–23). Because of his commitment to excellence and God's hand upon him, Joseph rose to power in a nation that had once enslaved him.

God does not promise to bless and help the lazy; rather, He has words to prod them to action (Proverbs 6:6–11; 10:4). But God is pleased with the diligent (Proverbs 10:3–4; 13:4;). Since God gives us His best in every way, we owe it to our Creator to pursue excellence in everything He's given us to do (Ecclesiastes 9:10).

3. Character; We attract Money by been intentional about our character. Character is defined as strength of moral fiber. A.W. Tozer described character as "the excellence of moral beings."

As the excellence of gold is its purity and the excellence of art is its beauty, so the excellence of man is his character. Persons of character are noted for their honesty, ethics, and charity.

Descriptions such as "man of principle" and "woman of integrity" are assertions of character. A lack of character is moral deficiency, and persons lacking character tend to behave dishonestly, unethically, and uncharitably.

A person's character is the sum of his or her disposition, thoughts, intentions, desires, and actions. It is good to remember that character is gauged by general tendencies, not on the basis of a few isolated actions. We must look at the whole life. For example, King David was a man of good character (1 Samuel 13:14) although he sinned on occasion (2 Samuel 11). And although King Ahab may have acted nobly once (1 Kings 22:35), he was still a man of overall bad character (1 Kings 16:33).

Several people in the Bible are described as having

noble character: Ruth (Ruth 3:11), Hanani (Nehemiah 7:2), David (Psalm 78:72), and Job (Job 2:3). These individuals' lives were distinguished by persistent moral virtue.

Character is influenced and developed by our choices. Daniel "resolved not to defile himself" in Babylon (Daniel 1:8), and that godly choice was an important step in formulating an unassailable integrity in the young man's life.

Character, in turn, influences our choices. "The integrity of the upright guides them" (Proverbs 11:3a). Character will help us weather the storms of life and keep us from sin (Proverbs 10:9a).

It is the Lord's purpose to develop character within us. "The crucible for silver and the furnace for gold, but the LORD tests the heart" (Proverbs 17:3). Godly character is the result of the Holy Spirit's work of sanctification.

Character in the believer is a consistent manifestation of Jesus in his life. It is the purity of heart that God gives becoming purity in action. God sometimes uses trials to strengthen character: "we also rejoice in our sufferings, because we know that suffering produces perseverance; perseverance, character; and character, hope" (Romans 5:3-4).

The Lord is pleased when His children grow in character. "You test the heart and are pleased with integrity" (1 Chronicles 29:17; see also Psalm 15:1-2).

We can develop character by controlling our thoughts (Philippians 4:8), practicing Christian virtues (2 Peter 1:5-6), guarding our hearts (Proverbs 4:23; Matthew 15:18-20), and keeping good company (1 Corinthians 15:33).

Men and women of character will set a good example for others to follow, and their godly reputation will be evident to all (Titus 2:7-8).Just know this that value attracts money, character multiply it and excellence manage it

4. Develop skills, competence and attention: It depends on who you are before the money follows. One has to be developed personally, concentrate on being the best version of yourself. It is based on who you are and not what you do you get money, one should grow and develop by so doing he gets power (power to take action, power to control the money). One should focus on improving themselves and the money will come naturally.

Financial intelligence is important. People tend to chase money without knowing the Dynamics of it, one needs to attract money by knowing and learning how it works. To get money is not easy and people think doing easy stuff will get them rich. One has to grow from the inside, work hard and the results will come later. It's not by doing easy things, one has to make sacrifices and pay for it with hard work, the end results will become easy (Life becomes easy).

The mindset of an individual is very important, you have to make up your mind to strive hard so as to rest later. The mindset is to focus on achieving difficult tasks and then easy task will be fixed later. With challenges comes success. you should be a master of a skill. They are different professions which can take years to master it but with skills it takes shorter period and you become a master of it. You need to choose the right skill to get positive results. To get to your destination one picks a vehicle that will be suitable for the journey so also skills, with the right skill in hand, you get your destination with positive results.If you are a master of any skill or field, you don't beg for money because the money follows you when you're good at what you do. Based on skills you are good;

having positive results, people will come to you naturally. To become a master takes competence, confidence; it takes patience, it doesn't happen in a day or month you work hard; keep learning; apply and grow in the skills continuously. Focus on it. Do not jump from one skill to another, let people know you are the master of that field. Take authority over it, you should be remembered for your field and to be remembered for your field you need to work hard. With competence comes money naturally. You needs to be courageous and also be bold to take hard steps. Leave your comfort zone and strive hard. you needs courage to market his products, you don't have to be very rich to be courageous. In whatever you do, be bold about it. you have to be committed to what he's doing. You shouldn't be off and on about your skill or business. We should always be consistent.

Whatever skills or business one is into, put in your best in it; be committed and consistent. From consistence comes competence and from competence comes mastery. Being committed leads to success of skills and business. You need to have a saving habit. Saving is very important in the aspect of money. One shouldn't squander money because he is having much today. You save money today, and it will save you tomorrow. Saving is an habit. You save to invest not to spend.

You shouldn't save money just to pile up cash but to make use of it to make more capitals. Money attracts more money. You save money before spending, decide to keep some percentage and after keeping the percentage; the remaining balance should be for spending. Earn more money and also save more!

It is important to invest money and multiply. The best way is to invest in yourself, even when there are challenges one bounce back easily. Invest your money on businesses, stocks and even real estate. Whatever you invest your money into, one should have a knowledge about it.

You should study the business, investigate on it and when satisfied with the results he can invest into it. You will always be wealthy when you invest your money. You should be with the right association. Been with you right associations attract great opportunities. Even when we don't have them as friends, hang out with them on social media (follow their handles and you get to see the things they do, how they go about their businesses; interviews and so much more).

You can learn from their actions and see how their mindsets works. Hang around people who are not broke and fly with the eagles. Leverage is important, using minimum efforts to get maximum results. With leverage, stuff are done the easy way with less energy. One doesn't have to start from the scratch use the available information and minimize your mistakes that use of Internet. Use the internet.

God bless you through people so you shouldn't look down on them. You should value every single relationship. Your connection can change your financial level. When you meet people, seek to add value to them first and you will gain favor when the time is right.

5. Prompt action - people have great ideas of business but claim they are waiting for the perfect time to start. When one has the idea ready for the business, start! You don't have to wait, get started with it and make corrections on the way. If one keeps waiting someone might end up doing your business idea. Knowledge is important so also action.

Action brings out distinction. Put whatever you learn into action and you get results from your acts. And this thing called Money will not be a mystery to you.

THE X SIMPLE PROCESS OF MAKING THIS THING CALLED MONEY

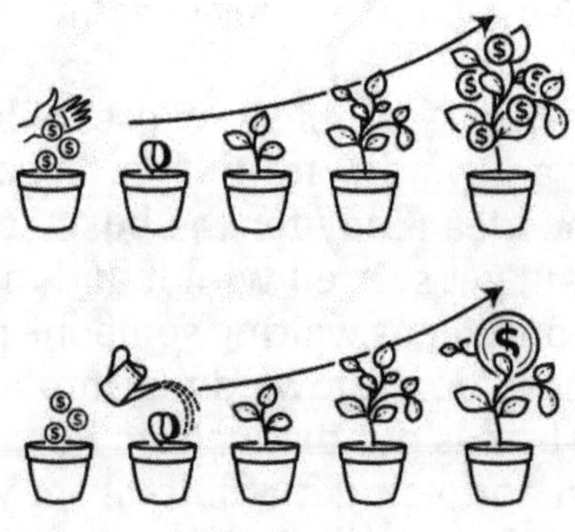

Chapter 10

THE X SIMPLE PROCESS OF MAKING
THIS THING CALLED
MONEY

Here is the thing.

Making a lot of money is a simple process that people always complicated.

I said Simple, Not easy.

It is about 2 things.

1. Have a product/service that solves a problem a lot of people have and are willing to pay to get rid of it. E.g. A couple who can't give birth want to get rid of that problem.
A woman who is overweight wants to get rid of that problem.
A business owner who is not making enough sales wants to get rid of that problem.

2. Have a distribution channel to get the product (solution) across to people who need it. This is where your knowledge about sales and marketing kicks in or you can just hire people who can do that work for you.

Now, if you can't create a product like most people, you can simply help people who have a good product with distribution. And everyone makes money and get rich.

Again, the main key that will really help you understanding is sales & marketing. Without sales, nothing happens. ***"Money is made by someone selling something to someone else."*** Just find something and be selling be it online or offline. Now think of this Doctors sells their high developed skills. Teachers, and course creators sells their time and teaching skills. Barbers, sells their Barbing skills. Comedians sells their humorous skills.

A Businessman think of money every time... Start business because of money but an Entrepreneur think of solving people's problem. Every entrepreneur is a businessman but not every businessman is an entrepreneur. Give them what they want and collect their money.

Action to take: Go get a book or a jotter, go out your street...town and find out what people desperately need and find solution... ASAP. And write in it those needs you discover and plan solutions.

CHAPTER *Eleven*

WHY GOD WANTS YOU TO HAVE THIS THING CALLED MONEY

WHY GOD WANTS YOU TO HAVE THIS THING CALLED
MONEY

God wants you to have money for three fundamental reasons:

To fund Kingdom work. To "go into all the world and preach the gospel" takes money!

To provide well for your own household. That's your job not your family's or the government's. God has called you to work to provide for yourself.

To subdue the earth. To have dominion on the earth, we should be controlling most of the resources. For example, if you don't like the immorality posted on the billboard outside your office, here is the answer: Own the billboard. If the magazines in the store are offensive: Own the magazines. That's how you subdue the earth.

Some denominations that claim we should not discuss money are often those whose members also work 80 hours each week to earn every dollar they can. On the other hand, many people in the faith camp are waiting for Publisher's Clearinghouse to show up on their doorstep rather than focusing on the spiritual role work plays in the manifestation of God's blessings.

BONUS *Chapter*

4 PRECISE PLACES TO INVEST THIS THING CALLED MONEY

4 PRECISE PLACES TO INVEST THIS THING CALLED MONEY

Start investing NOW!

Before I tell you the 4 ways to invest your money lets discuss about diversifying your Investments.

Ecclesiastes 11:2- "Invest in seven ventures, yes, in eight; you do not know what disaster may come upon the land." Investing your money in several different types of assets helps to protect your money. It smoothen out your returns and minimizes risk vs. keeping all your investments in one asset.

I'm sure you've heard the old phrase, "don't put all your eggs in one basket". This is an excellent example of great biblical investing principle at work.

Why Should You Diversify Your Investments?

Spreading your investments over different types of assets keeps you from being overly dependent on the performance of one type of asset. If the value of one type of asset tanks for a while, other assets may do better.

For instance, at least once a decade or so, my stock market investments drop 20-40% due to economic conditions. But when that happens, my rental property is still going up in value and generating income every month!

Here's a short list of assets you can use to diversify your portfolio:

* Single stocks
* Mutual funds
* ETF's

* Real estate
* Gold
* Bonds
* Money lending
* Business ventures
* And hundreds more...

Don't Hoard Your Wealth
Ecclesiastes 5:13-14- "I have seen a grievous evil under the sun: wealth hoarded to the harm of its owners, or wealth lost through some misfortune, so that when they have children there is nothing left for them to inherit."

Luke 16:9- "I tell you, use worldly wealth to gain friends for yourselves, so that when it is gone, you will be welcomed into eternal dwellings."

I once heard a saying that "money is like manure, it's only good if you spread it around." It's a great thing to invest money and build huge amounts of wealth, but you should never keep it all to yourself. Hoarded money is a sign of a stagnant soul. Now the 4 strategic way to invest.

1. **Invest in yourself**: This looks so simple and common sense but most people don't do it. The most important investment you can ever make is the investment in yourself.

This is the only investment that can truly guarantee you 1000% returns.

Why's that?
The better you become, the more money you can make. Every other can be stolen from you but the investment in self cannot be taken away.

Most people don't know that more money follows competence, courage and consistency. The better you become, the more money you can make.

2. Learn a high income skill: Yes, you can still learn the basics of a high-income before the year is out. There is a difference between a high income job (like shell), a high income profession (like Medicine) and a high income skill (like copywriting)

The first two requires longer time, training and resources. The last one can be learnt in months and the rewards are equal.

Believe it or not, there are programmers (high income skill) who earn a lot more than lawyers (high income profession)

My advice number is, learn a high income skill that can help you fetch more money. Invest in courses and training.

3. Create daily streams of income from your Ventures :Daily streams of income are businesses that bring in cash on a daily basis. Even if it is 1k a day, it is better than nothing or waiting at the end of the month.

If you don't find a way to make money daily, poverty will find a way to meet you daily.

The most common daily streams of income are selling digital products in the form of eBooks, courses and videos or training people online.

I have 3 daily streams of income. I sell digital products, Invest in creating a digital product or reselling one that works.

4. Start a supplementary business: Supplementary businesses are businesses you start by leveraging an already existing business or traffic.

For example and this is very basic, if someone is selling akara, partner with them so that they can sell bread on your behalf. That's just the idea.

Look for where the traffic is and leverage on it. It is a

model I've used over and over to reap passive streams of income.

5.   Invest in an agency Business: If you have a skill and you know how to get clients easily, gather a people, train them and let them work for you.
   *   This is what Ushering agencies do.
   *   This is what writing agencies do.
   *   Same thing security agencies do.
   *   What can you bring people together and offer? Invest in it.

Conclusion

THIS THING CALLED
MONEY

Conclusion
THIS THING CALLED
MONEY

Health and family are some of the most important things in life. If you have those two things, then you are living a pretty rich life. But there is no denying the importance of money and that it can create better life opportunities.

Naturally, money won't solve all your problems and if you were an unhappy person prior to money, then gaining some wealth may only be a temporary solution. The real opportunity is to find the right balance where you see money as important, but a tool that can help you create better life experiences and opportunities.

Money is one subject that has a sense of irony attached to it. People can't pretend that they don't need money or need the secret to succeed in life. People spend all their entire lives working to get money. Yet, they behave as if getting money is something that is either evil or is of little importance.

So I leave you with this gist, Do you know that all over the world today God is raising up a new breed wealth builder who will use their money to shape world history. Without building a Golden calf. I may not have really have a full test of wealth and prosperity like the world may think of but I do know that true prosperity is not about having houses and cars rather it's about influence and impact building wealth is not just for you, its to affect our entire families, cities, nations and atmosphere. It's not about naming it and claiming it, it's about selfishness and greed.

Its about you never having to ask money for

permission to obey God or do what is in your heart. It's about funding your life mission and making your greatest impact. It's about leaving an inheritance to your children's children.

It's about provision for your vision.

It's time...it's your time. Listen there is no prosperity gospel in the Bible. But the gospel of the kingdom does include prosperity. God is removing the hype and the facade. God never said he would just give you wealth. But he did give you the power to create wealth.

And the goodnews is that you can grow wealth with God regardless of your age, income or experience.

Today, there are so many people teaching you about Money and how God wants you to prosper and that's absolutely true. But not many people are teaching you how to prosper. I believe now that you've gone through this book: "This thing Called Money" you now have a glimpse as to why having Money is important and you also have a big picture of what it means to have it and striking a balance with your spirituality.

Remember, Money is not evil but the love of it. There are reasons God wants you to prosper and have this thing called Money. It's a daily necessity whether we like it or not.

God is raising an army and he desperately wants you to be part of it. It's time for you to take your place. It's time for you to create the provision for your vision. It time for you to fund your life mission and make your greatest impact and remember, affluence is for influence. Income is for impact. MONEY HAS A PURPOSE.

Blessings,
Your Brother,
Godson Gode Dauda.

BIBLIOGRAPHY

Abodunde, Ayodeji Elton's role as length in messenger: Sydney Elton and the making of Pentecostalism in Nigeria, Lagos; Pierce Watershed, 2016.

Adeleye, Femi Preachers of a Different Gospel Nairobi; WordAlive publishers, 2011

Bakker, Jim, in an interview with Charisma February 1997

Bowler, Catherine Blessed: A History of the American Prosperity Gospel, Dissertation submitted in partial fulfillment of the requirements for the degree of Doctor of Philosophy in the Graduate Program in Religion in the Graduate School of Duke University, 2010.

Copeland, Gloria God's will is Prosperity, Forth Worth, Kenneth Copeland publications, 1978

Copeland, Kenneth The Laws of Prosperity, Tulsa (OK), Harrison House, 1974.

Francis, Kelly Joseph The World of the Early Christians Liturgical Press, 1997.

Goff, J. The Faith that Claims, in Christianity Today, n. 34, February 1990.

Hill, H. How to be a Winner, Alachua (FL), Bridge Logos, 1976.

Hinn, Costi God, Greed and the (prosperity) gospel, Michigan; Zondervan, 2019.

Kenyon, The Two Kinds of Faith: Faith's Secret Revealed Lynnwood, WA: Kenyon's Gospel Publishing Society, 1998.

Lake, John G. Spiritual Hunger and Other Sermons, ed. Gordon Lindsay Dallas: Christ for the Nations, 1994

MacConnell, D. R. A Different Gospel, Peabody, MA: Hendrickson publishers, 1988.

Maxey, S. Gary and Ozodo Peter, The Seduction of the Nigerian Church, Lagos: WATS publications, 2017.

McKeown, James Genesis Two Horizons; Grand Rapids, MI: Eerdmans, 2008.

Oyedepo, David O. Success System Ikeja; Dominion publishing house, 2006.

Oyedepo, David O. Covenant Wealth Lagos; Dominion publishing House, 1992.

Perrotta, Cosimo, Consumption as an Investment: The fear of goods from Hesiod to Adam Smith, Psychology Press, 2004.

Sproul, R. C. Everyone's a Theologian, an Introduction to

Systematic Theology, Michigan; Ligonier Ministries, 2014.

Ukpong, Justice S. The Problem of God and Sacrifice in African Traditional Religion Journal Article published by Brill, 1983.

BIBLES

Barker, Kenneth L. ed., NIV study Bible Michigan, Zondervan, 1920

Barton, Bruce B. ed. Life Application Study Bible Wheaton, Illinois; Tyndale House Publishers, 1989.

Grudem, Wayne, Global study Bible Illinois; crossway wheaton, 2012

Sproul, R. C. ed. The Reformation Study Bible Orlando, Florida; Reformation Trust, 2014.

Dictionaries, Commentaries and Encyclopedias

Alexander, B. S. Rosner; Downers Grove, IL/Leicester: IVP, 2000.

Brand, Chad ed. Holman Illustrated Bible Dictionary Nashville, Tennessee; Holman Bible publishers, 2003.

Evans, Mary J. "Blessing, Curse" in New Dictionary of Biblical Theology eds. T D

JOURNALS

Nelson, Tebb, The Journal of Religion; inheritance and disinheritance; African customary law and constitutional right, Published by the university of Chicago press, 2008.

INTERNET SOURCES

Barrier, Roger How Many Times Should I Pray Healing Prayers www.preachitteachit.org, retrieved 8/6/2020.

Bouma, Jeremy Paul have five things to say to rich Christians www.zondervanacademic. Com retrieve 7/27/2020.

Bowler, Kate Death, the prosperity gospel and me, www.nytimes.com retrieved 7/28/20.

Cole, Stecen J. Lesson 19: why Christians must be truthful (Colossians) (3 John 1-15)

___________, Lesson 3: The Prosperous Soul (3 John 1-15) www.bible.org, retrieved 8/8/20.

___________, Are Deeds a Better Sign of Love Than words? (www.desiringgod.org), retrieved 8/9/2020.

Copeland, Kenneth what is prosperity www.Kcm.org accessed 3/25/2020.

Davidson, Roy How Can We Know the Truth? www.oldpaths.com, assessed 8/8/20

Graham, Bill Love in action www.faithgate.com, retrieved 8/9/20.

Guzik, David 3 John- Following Good Examples, www.enduringword.com retrieved 8/8/2020.

Hinn, Costi W. The Prosperity Gospel: A Global Epidemic, www.reformandamin.org accessed 3/26/20.

http://www.biblebasedmedicine.com/a-brief-history-of-the-prosperity-gospel.html

https://billmuehlenberg.com/2014/06/10/warnings-about-riches-old-testament retrieved 6/27/2020.

https://medium.com/@anthonymays/what the gospel really says about prosperity retrieved 6/27/2020.

https://www.bbc.co.uk bitesize guides zkw2vk7 revision 8, Jesus teaching retrieved 7/22

https://www.zakat.org/en/five-essential-islamic-teachings-on-wealth
Jones, David W. http://intersectproject.org faith-and-economics/what did Jesus really

Laurie, Greg https://www.christianity.com/jesus/life-of-jesus/teaching-and-

Lowrance, Carrie 10 Christians Virtues We Need to Revive www.crosswalk.com, retrieved 8/8/20.

Matthew Henry's 3 John 1 Bible commentary

www.christinaity.com, retrieved 8/8/20.

Messages/what-did-Jesus-teach-about-wealth. retrieved 7/23/2020.

Piper, John prospeority preaching: deceitful and deadly www.desiringgod.org, 14/2/2007.

Pollock, DennisProsperity, Abundance, and Paul https://www.spiritofgrace.org/articles retrieved 7/27/2020

Prosperity www.dictionary.com accessed 3/25/2020.

Ps://biblehub.com retrieved 23/3/20120.

Reeves, Keith https://oikonomianetwork.org/2015/04/ the-testaments-treat-wealth-differently retrieved 6/27/2020.

Roos, Dave How the Prosperity Gospel Works www.people.howstuffworks.com. retrieved 7/28/2020

The concept of wealth in Islam www.thestar.com retrieved 7/29/20.

The prosperity gospel, explained: why Joel Osteen believes that prayer can make you rich, www.vox.com, retrieved 7/28/20.